LOVING YOU

LOVING YOU

A Journey of Love
Through Poetry

BY

Vicki Reneé

The Book Tree
San Diego

Loving You
A Journey of Love Through Poetry
© 2008
by Vicki Reneé

Cover art by Rassouli
Cover layout & design: Atulya
Interior layout and design: Atulya

ISBN 978-1-58509-33-1

Printed in USA on Acid-Free Paper

DEDICATION

I can shed tears that he is gone. Or I can smile that he
has lived. My heart can be empty because I can not see him
physically. Or I can be full of love that we shared. I can
turn my back on tomorrow and live in yesterday. Or I can
be happy for tomorrow because of OUR yesterdays. I can
remember him and only that he is gone. Or I can cherish
his memory and let it live on. I can cry and close my mind,
be empty and turn my back or I can do what he would
want. smile, laugh, open my eyes, love totally, live on and
honor our love. Know he is still with me and feel his love
from above.

Table of Contents

INTRODUCTION

This series of poems is the story of a person who was both fortunate and able to find a twin spirit in this lifetime. That person is me. I feel I am blessed to have kept track of my journey with Tim through words and poems. His love and devotion to me, and I to him, was expressed through heartfelt verse as it unfolded and now, after having assembled it chronologically, I can appreciate and validate it daily. There are others who may be as fortunate, or those who wish to experience some of the soulful emotion involved in this journey. This book is for those who have found a perfect love and lost it, who understand or wish to understand how a small piece of heaven can be found on the Earth, and how one can at least try to heal from the aftermath of a tragic loss.

Of course all was not completely perfect during our time together. There were bumps and rocks in our life and our love. Despite this we were able to accept one another as perfect and divine souls that fit together in a way that we knew was "meant to be." He was and is my everything. He completed me. I would stare at him and he would ask what I was doing. I would answer, "Taking a picture with my heart." I did not realize at the time that this was such an important thing to do.

I hope you will relate to my words. They were all real. This book itself was a journey of its own - while being assembled it brought out the original emotions once again, allowing and sometimes forcing me to relive the experience. The idea of allowing others to look into my life was hard. Then I realized that others may identify with it, or have the words identify with them and their beloved. This book was made to show how one person, not just me, can love another so much. I lost the love of my life, however, and the joy I had was followed by pain. What can I do? What can anyone do?

People should have a relationship with their own true self. It involves the love, joy and sometimes pain which accompanies a total love in your life. The emotions expressed within this book are very deep and personal, and trust they will resonate with those who have traveled a similar path or are currently on one. Know you are a treasured blessing and I pray that you enjoy my words and that they touch your heart.

Vicki Reneé

FINDING LOVE

My soul's reflection in a mirror.
It happens once in a lifetime,
that spark, that fire, those ever consuming flames,
when the soul and the soul meet face-to-face.

You

He came out of nowhere
to look upon my eyes
with such strength and honor
his touch was not a lie.

He was so virile
yet fragile to the core
and in remembrance
he left me wanting more.

He was so beautiful
a picture of perfect health,
no amount of money could buy him,
no amount of wealth.

Just before I left
I gazed upon him with my heart.
He had been the only one,
what a priceless work of art.

My Soul's Reflection

I am consistently walking the halls of wonder,
amazed at its many treasures,
undaunted at life's tasks, its wants and needs
to provide him of my pleasures.
To find the love that has managed to elude me,
and confuse me till the shyness corrupts me to wait,
but with diligent effort, and spiritual guidance
I too, can find my soul's mate.
A speck in the distance, so small an alluring
I travel in time ever nearer,
seeing signs of match made with God's own hands,
my soul's reflection in a mirror.
It happened once in a lifetime,
that spark, that fire, those ever consuming flames,
when the soul and the soul meet face-to-face,
cleansed of all of wrong one's blames.
To grow old as one, to pass on to future generations
that yes, it can be done,
as long as we search though good times and bad,
the heart has already won.

In You

Just as the bird finds its freedom in the air
high above the world's troubles,
I find my freedom in you;

Just as the sun shines brightly with its ray of warmth,
even on the murkiest of days,
I find my warmth in you.

Just as the oceans are deep, alive, and full,
I find my love deep, my soul alive,
my heart full in you.

Just as one finds tranquility in the soft touch and
the gentle whispers of the silence,
I find my tranquility in you.

Just as we all go throughout our lives
searching for our destiny,
I find my destiny in you.

In the Distance

Across the room I look to find,
the most intriguing man within my sight.
His demeanor was captivating,
his smile was alluring.
Long before I knew it,
my heart was voracious,
begging to appreciate
what was so glorious.

I soon surrendered to his temptation,
and devoured a pleasure of resurrection.
Thanks to him I experienced,
the most unspeakable elevation.
Because of our obligations
we went our separate ways,
but our hearts stayed together,
in the distance far away.
His memory will live
with me forever,
a desire I will long for
and always measure.

Thou Art

Fragile wings of the dawn
unfold all around me
as I watch the darkness
split apart by the light.

I catch the tendrils
of thought
on my fingertips
then send them
soaring high into the sky.

Chase dewdrops
of the morning,
chase the songs
of the doves,
chase the dying light
of the morning star,
then come to me,
my hearts delight.

Thou art
fairer than the dawn

sweeter than the summer,
softer than the cool breeze
that blows through the heated trees.

Thou art
gentler than the rain,
patient as springtime,
filling my heart with wonder
after the chill of wintertime.

Thou art
Light
to my dying vision.
Pure glory,
Rapture,
In your presence I believe.

Thou art
Beloved,
dearer than mere mortal;
king and the keeper
of my heart that clings to thee.

The Mockingbird

Lovely is the Mockingbird
whose song trills through the dawn,
I glance at treetops and pecked roofs
to find the one he's on.

He seems to know my heart
is bursting with love
and he sings to praise this wonderment
as reigns in from above.

I sense the night's retreat from day
as I sip my tepid tea,
a strawberry-kiwi,
soothing as can be.

The stars fade this tapestry
to become a silken blue,
as I have
another sip of tea with you.

The day will come, rest assured
our paths will be as one.
Tea will be a shared event
while waiting for the sun.

I pray I never take for granted
such love as you have shown,
so many slip into the rut when
love becomes their own.

They cannot recall the broken dreams
that woke them in the night
nor hold onto the waking
dreams, when all is shown in light.

I want to be your only love,
truth which can't be lost.
I hope and pray you find my heart
worthy of love's cost.

The Journey

Let's go under the stars
you and I.
Arms around each other
on the lake,
at daybreak
above our laughter,
hear the birds.

Let's look at the sun,
rejoicing
warming our faces;

Let's walk together toward the park
where the trees stretch forever
in a summer beyond the seasons.

I want you with me through eternity.

Unfolding

I am unfolding gently beneath
your loving touch.
Becoming.
I let wholeness breath my
petals free.
Awareness.
Sweet fragrant Spirit touching
senses into life.
Wisdom.
Giving beauty back to the universe.
Knowing.
Each petal, sweet miracle of life.
Oneness
We are hues of color, yet one
in Spirit's blossom.

His Life

He came into this life
on his own accord,
the world was mystic for him,
he lived with nature;
he lived with neon;
the world was his playground.
He played too much,
until the angels came down
and kissed each eye shut.
And now he belongs to them;
now may he play without
torment.

Come

Come,
touch the things you
cannot feel.
Come,
open your eyes to the
things you cannot see.
Come,
feel what you've never
felt before.
Come,
my soul is
open to you.

Shy Angel

Lonely, shy, with timid care,
strangers meeting in the night.
Reaching out for one to share,
one to walk with in the light.
Years I've waited, in control;
searching for stability.
Sky blue mirrors of your soul
set my love and feelings free.
Long forgotten dreams arise;
needing love, afraid to start.
When I gaze into your eyes
tender looks will heal my heart.
Angel, come into my life
with your eyes of Summer hue.
Be my lover and my life;
I am on my knees for you.
Stay with me from year to year,
love will grow each day and hour.
Now I know it's true love, dear,
I'm lost within your power.

The Promise

The promise of love sustains me,
not a love for a lonely man,
nor a kiss mired in sympathy,
but a love of totality.

The crispness of infatuation
working the miracle in me,
the longing for ruptured bliss
sealing my fate with a soulful kiss.

I willingly go with an open heart,
to a world that seems so cruel.
I hold out my hand for someone to touch me,
Exposed...

ADMIRATION

If you said I was a flower,
I would bloom before you, paint my throat
with pollen, weave my purple hair into
velvet petals, curled to crimson at the edges.

A Thousand Words

A thousand words upon a page
cannot bestow as much
as a simple line of poetry,
nor give so sweet a touch.
A glittering field of fallen snow
can never mystify
as a simple crystal snowflake
that stays etched within the eye.
A universe of stars above
cannot evoke delight
as a single candle glowing
in the blackness of the night.
A book is like a treasure chest
to open up the mind;
a poem settles in the soul
and stays the rest of time.

Wanting You

I still treasure those first few moments when your eyes met mine.
Wondrous thoughts that filled my being appeared to me a sign.
But without the give and take of love those thought have fled.
Now I feel our new love is all but dead.

Loneliness is bearing down, yet no one seems to care.
Filled with love, my heart overflowing, no one wants to share.
Chance encounters, no commitments, wanting just a friend.
Heart and soul reach out to offer loving without end.

Can you not accept me as your lover or your mate?
Or should friends and lovers just be left to chance and fate?
Never freely showing your emotions kept inside,
Love in eyes and heart on sleeve, it's something that can't hide.

Rose Buds and Roses

Is a rose more beautiful than its bud?
Are all rosebuds meant to be roses?

The history of a rose as a rosebud
does not detract from it's beauty as a rose.

The future of a rosebud as a rose
Does not lessen it's unique
magnificence as a rosebud.

I love you for what you are,
not what you were or will be.
What you are is now.

I Would Do these Things

If you said I was a flower,
I would bloom before you, paint my throat
with pollen, weave my purple hair into
velvet petals curled to crimson at the edges,
scent my graceful shoulders with
the sweet perfume of summer,
unfurl strips of thin green leaves and
pin them to my hips,
sink my feet into the soil and point
my toes in all directions;
If you said I was a flower.

Leave

I am powerless.
You come near with that look in your eye,
with that smile on your face,
you twist me around your finger.
Your arms wrap around me.
Your breath is so close,
I can taste you.

There is a pain in your soul,
pain in your eye.
You lift me so high,
then you left me to die.
You take me to the heavens,
then you leave me there,
as if you don't even care.

Do you see inside me?
Please see how I feel.
Do you see that you are tearing me apart?
Can you even sense the love I have for you?
Do you see how you let me?
Do you see how you left me to die?

Leave before you destroy me;
leave before I am dead.
Take away the knife in your kiss,
before it has cut me to shreds.

Helpless I am, living under the glass,
as I see you so far and so near.
You reach out and touch,
then you go on your way,
while you drop on the road, the heart that I gave.
Don't you see me, so empty and bruised?
Or have you even looked?

Leave before you destroy me,
leave before I am dead.
Take away the knife of your kiss,
before it has cut me to shreds.

Seasons

Spring is where life begins,
the seasons cycle starts anew.
I have experienced rebirth,
for I have discovered you.

Summer is the time of beauty,
love is felt the whole day though.
We grew and now we bind together,
for now I know you love me, too.

Fall will be the promised harvest
when we can love the whole night through,
pledging mutual alliance,
angels blessings my love to you.

Winter's chill approaches,
the seasons growth is through,
I will take leave to thank my maker
for allowing me to worship you.

Did I Ever Tell You

Did I ever tell you
how very much I love you?
That the mere sight of you
weakens me to my very soul?

Did I ever tell you
how very much I want you?
That I would feel the
world had come to an end
if I could not have you?

Did I ever tell you
how very much I hunger for you?
That you are so tender with my emotions
and would never want to hurt me?

Yet beyond all that
you've allowed me to trust again,
to be supported by you when things
get bad
and most of all, you loved me back.

Take Love with You

On this night I give you
my love you know is true.
I want you to take this
when you have to go,
and always remember me, too.
Take this tear and tuck it tight;
If you hold it close
it will keep you warm at night.
Take this smile I have for you;
Only know of my heart
I keep you in a special place,
from which you will not depart.
Take this gentle kiss I blow;
Keep it with you at all times.
Remember it when you look at the stars
and watch as the brightest one shines.
When you get to feeling lonely,
close your eyes and dream

of a far away place,
you know the one I mean.
Sit a while under the apple tree,
feel the wind blow on your face,
hear the soft whisper of a butterfly's pace.
See the golden apple as it dangles from above,
only let it remind you of happiness and love.
So if you must go now,
don't let it bring you down.
I will always be with you,
I won't let you down.
I'll hold your hand and go with you,
If you keep my love.
Take it with you when you go,
never forget to look above.
See the stars and the moon,
see the sun so bright,
know that any given day or even any night,
I'll be thinking of you, and hoping you're all right.

I Love You with All I Am

I love you with all I am
and all I'll ever be.
You are my moon, my sun and stars,
My earth, my sky, my sea.

My love for you goes down and down
beneath both life and death,
so deep it must remain when I
have drawn my last faint breath.

Holding you for months and years
will make time disappear,
will make your lips my lips, your face
my face, your tear my tear;
will make us one strange personage
all intertwined in bliss,
not a man or woman, live or dead—
just nothing-but a kiss!

SOUL CONNECTION

Silently I've told you my life story
gently I've whispered my love.
Did you feel the swaying of our souls,
as they methodically unite?

A Soul to Give

He completes me;
all the things I love, he loves.
Too many thoughts to recite in verse,
but he mends my broken Shakespeare
when my tortured tongue attempts to write.
His voice is pure and sweet
as he sings to my spirit and to my soul;
beautiful too, yet dangerous,
with silk-smooth hair, and pallid cheek,
I gape in awe, and tell of only the lesser part.

I ache too much when he is gone,
counting minutes, hours and seconds
until he calls, or writes, or passes by.
Strange, it is a happy hurt,
as I know the comfort of his arms,
Time and sweet-soft silence together
in dreams so tender, holding his heart.
I am his to have, and his love is mine.

I wasn't looking for affection,
but he found me, and I cherish him
as never another in all my days
and this sensation, too, is new.

How can I tell
what it is to wake and live,
after sleep has stolen a dozen years,
with the self-same guilt, and hidden tears?

Strange, how slight traces of him
put a small and silly smile upon my face.
I detect his scent when he is gone,
and taste his lips in dreams, as awake.
His picture waits, and holds for me
patiently there, in and through my mind.

My life before seemed so unreal;
as another's life, and I am a witness.
Now the moments seem so true,
I feel, grasp, and take my being.
Once again I think, feel and share.

The sharing is the most important part,
for love is dead when two souls part.
This is what it means to live,
to share our lives; two hearts to give.

Beautiful Moment

From behind the pine trees she'll appear,
walking down a daisy-lined path,
on her beloved's arm,
never will there be a
more beautiful moment for me.

A vision in ivory moving toward him,
their eyes meeting in a smile,
he sings the song he wrote for her,
never will there be a
more beautiful moment for them.

The sunlight falls between the leaves,
as the wind blows softly through her hair,
they vow their love and devotion,
never will there be a
more beautiful moment.

If This was a Movie

If this was a movie
we'd look into each others eyes
and fall in love.
If this were a novel
I could turn the page
and know your thoughts.
If we were the two main characters
of any given romance
we'd be destined for each other.
But life isn't scripted;
things don't happen
to achieve maximum dramatic effect.
God doesn't care about
plot considerations,
and happy endings.
They are only found in fiction
because in real life
no one cares,
and the credits
Never
Roll.

Heaven's Door

He comes,
with soft knowing eyes.
I have seen his face
a thousand times and more.

He wakes me
silently,
kisses both my eyes.
His breath is garden.
His skin flowers.

I am not afraid.
As long as he is with me,
air is pink.
Clouds are cotton.
All is gentle.
He holds me close,
rocks me like a baby,
breeze is warm.

He takes my hand
saying,
Come
With
Me.

Reunion

To see where this life just might lead,
his heaven is mine,
my light is all his.
For no love could keep him away.
Again.
As winter approaches
we dance together again
with tears in our eyes,
on this blissful bridge of sighs.
Our winters together we shall spend
just loving each other,
it must be to survive
and is the life we both want to see.
She kissed him goodbye,
he kissed her hello.
We will never give up our dream.
He then became absent,
I hoped he would find me.
In my life I passionately miss him.
And with a smile and a reason
he came back into my life,
with a love, a kiss, and a whisper.
He says we will always meet again.

Love

The strongest feeling known for us humans is to love.
This feeling can make us go anywhere to find that One.
No distance is too great, no problem is too much to overcome.
The fire inside me burns with a strong flame
The flame of love is burning, the flame of love is pure
That burns only for you.
I think of you every waking minute and when I sleep
you are there, inside me all the time.
My heart belongs to you and only you.
I think of your eyes, your lips, your nose, your hair,
your ears, your arms, your fingers, your legs, your toes.
I think about all of you, all the time.
I love every part of you, I love your voice, your laughter,
your thoughts, your worries, your smiles, your hopes.

I want to be a part of your life,
to be there to share the up and downs,
that life is full of.
I want to comfort you when
you're sad, brush the tears away when you cry.
I care for you and want to make you happy,
I want you to shine as the sun does every morning,
I want to put a red rose every morning on your pillow,
I want you to know that my heart only burns for you,
that you are the light of my life, and you are very loved.
I just want you to know this-my feelings for you.
Go beyond this earth out into the universe.
It's the same thing with my love for you,
I'll be there for you, my love.

Fell in Love

Transcending all standards
ignoring all "norms"
I am drawn to you.
I see beyond all appearance
far enough to see your soul.
Timeless,
ageless,
I fell in Love.

First Light

You came into the darkened,
innermost chambers of my heart.
The light of your Spirit
illuminated every shadow.

You opened my eyes
to an Eternal Light that had been shining,
but not seen before I met you.

Your gentle spirit cradled my vulnerability,
accepted my weaknesses,
and guided me to wholeness.

There's a Miracle

There's a Miracle
happening here
for everyday
I've been more sure
that
out of the chaos
of this world
the Hand of God
brought me to you.

Visions

When I close my eyes
it is you I see,
when I lay my head down at night
it is you I dream.

When I feel my heart beat
it is you that calms,
when I ask God why he put you here
He answers, "For you my dear."

The Light of Our Dreams

The times of our longings pass quickly,
loving as one being,
seeing the glow
in the light of our dreams.
Time flows with the ebb of the moon,
and the sun rises on our love.
Time moves with the pace
of our joy.
The movement of our feelings
is in time with the tempo of the universe.
Our love moves in time,
with our passions and hopes,
vibrations and spirits to guide us.
Lovers and seers alike
make time for each other
being in the movement
thus feeling the heavenly light.

Is the act and virtue of our loving?
Our journey is the time of life.
The time of life is the loving.
Memories we cherish
with the glowing of passion,
knowing time is all we have.
Seeing you now in my heart,
my love, my feeling.
To know I can't lose you
ever again in life and love
and the hope we feel for each other.
Knowing I have always loved you,
in knowing you I always will.
Is the greatest passion of life and loving.
That glows with
the light of our dreams.

Union

As you lay sleeping last night,
I felt your breath on my cheek.
I know I have felt it before,
but there was something about it
that made it feel like the first time.

It was uneven at first, but then
as you fell deeper into sleep,
it became rhythmical and magical.
It was as though you were touching me
with your breath.

I lay still for a long time,
listening to the soft sound of your breath
and feeling the steady pressure
on my cheek.

On an impulse I moved my head slightly
so that I could breath in the air

as it touched my face.
It didn't occur to me for a while
that you were taking in my breath.

Tiny molecules from deep inside you
came into me and passed back into your body.
Each of them must have been charged
with the energy of our hopes and dreams,
disappointments, sorrows and love.

Love provides union,
while making room for separateness.

Union nourishes wholeness,
and depends on uniqueness.

Wholeness cradles our broken parts,
and blends them into the tapestry of our lives.

Before I was Myself You made Me, Me

Before I was myself you made me, me,
with love and patience, discipline and tears,
then bit by bit, stepped back to set me free,
allowing me to sail upon my sea,
though well within the headlands of your fears.

Before I was myself you made me, me,
with dreams of what I wanted to be,
and hopes that would be sculpted by the years,
then bit by bit, stepped back to set me free,
relinquishing your powers gradually,
to let me shape myself among my peers.

Before I was myself you made me, me,
and being good and wise, you gracefully stood by
as a dancer, when the last sweet cadence nears,
bit by bit, you stepped back to set me free.

For love inspires learning naturally.
The mind assents to what the heart reveres.
So it was through love you made me, me.
By slowly stepping back to set me free.

My Soul

When you look at me deeply
you take away my breath.

You can see inside my soul
it is pure for you.
I lived without you up until now,
yet how will I be able to leave your arms again?

My soul has waited a long time for yours,
and you have my permission to share it with me.
My heart has been yours
for some time now,
for which you will never leave.
I promise I will keep you safe and warm
even when we are apart.

Silently

Silently I've told you my life story,
gently I've whispered, my love.
Did you feel the swaying of our souls,
as they methodically unite?

LOVE MAKING

Rising to hold, encompassed by music's tender shroud,
glowing fires cast bewitching shadows,
a lover's waltz blissfully shimmering on bare walls.
Exhausted we fall together.

After the Love

Exhausted, we lie there
both spent from our passions.
Hands touching, caressing
the paths of our kisses.

The fluttering heartbeat
subsides from near bursting,
ebbs slowly each minute,
to intertwined sleep.

Perhaps there to dream of
our intimate pleasure.
Through love we have given
sweet memories to keep.

Warm comforting closeness
awakens beside me.
My love, my best friend.

He Sleeps

So softly by my side – he sleeps.
The love I feel – so real.
My fingers gently travel
the highways of his face.
Don't awaken.
I want to etch this in my mind – forever.
I breathe him in.
I watch his hands – memorizing,
they twitch in silent dreams.
I hope I am there with him,
behind his gently fluttering eyes.
My own eyes close now,
I can still taste his flavor,
my skin still tingles where
it has been loved.
Softly by my side,
now softly in my mind
he sleeps.
Near the red petals of my lips.

He is Magic

He is a diamond amongst the sands of manhood,
cut to perfection by the Gods.
His companionship projecting an ordinary man
to the envy of all mankind.

By chance we meet, gorgeous eyes burrow into my heart,
holding me spellbound.
A candle flickers though red wine, reflecting his mood,
charting a journey to my soul.

Rising to hold, encompassed by music's tender shroud,
glowing fires cast bewitching shadows,
a lover's waltz blissfully shimmering on bare walls.
Exhausted we fall together.

As firelight licks our bodies, we tenderly embrace,
creating tempests of passion
and rising up to glorious heights of human spirit,
I inject my soul into his soft frame.

Laying his sweet head gently on silken pillows,
so stunning in slumber.
Kissing his lips, whispering love, affection,
yearning to protect him.

Unworthy of his eternal beauty, I depart
desperate to return.
Dream, my lover, in your solitary chamber,
I am with you always.

Dearest One

Dearest One:
Suffocate me in your beauty.
Sing to me in your splendor.
Imprison me in your passion.
Lock me in my words.
Free me to the Infinite.
Walk with me in movement forward.
Now I am alive!

Poerotica

A musk-scented rose
I lay at your feet,
kneeling down
so I may look into your eyes.

Taking the rose
in my teeth,
I will await the nod
of your acceptance,
then I will rise
into the arms
of your love.

I Tremble

When your soft skin
caresses my flesh
I Tremble.
When your strong arms
embrace my body
I Tremble.
When your sweet kisses
brush my lips
I Tremble.
When your yearning eyes
look through my heart
I Tremble.
When your loving heart
touches my soul.

END IN SIGHT

Stain these vacant walls with your song,
hit them hard and leave your mark.
Throw your rainbow to the floor,
let it soak and seep into the grains.
I will paint myself
into your portrait.
A twisted memory.

God Knew

God knew that you were suffering,
that the hills were hard to climb,
so He gently closed your eyelids
and whispered "Peace be thine."
In tears we watched you sinking,
we watched you fade away.
Our hearts were surely broken,
you fought so hard to stay.

But when we saw you sleep
so peaceful, free from pain,
we could not wish you back
to suffer that again.
It broke our hearts to lose you
but you did not go alone,
for part of us went with you,
the day God called you home.

The Land He Walked In

There is a timeless Land Tim walked in without fear.
The stars were his night lights.
He wandered there through valleys of galaxies.
The suns and moons knew his name.

Now and again he journeyed the path of pain in time.
In quiet moments an unknown nostalgia
reminded him that he was visiting a small
corner of another Land he walked in.

The Land he walked in called to him with
an intensity that he only slightly understood.

Just a Little Longer

Desolation,
wide open space,
between the trees and me.
Emptiness and me.
Confusion and decisions,
feelings hard to define,
and I say to myself,
Just a little longer.

Coldness seeps
its way in,
I am falling deeper,
into what I fear most.
As I reach out,
there is nothing there,
it's possible there was something once,
only to be gone,
and I say to myself,
Just a little longer.

The sun drops,
the last inch of light falls,
the squirrels are more likely to be huddled up,
but not me.
A warmth I could never possess,
and I say to myself,
Just a little longer.

Then the sun has gone,
darkness spreads its wings over me.
I see nothing so no one sees me.
Feeling of bitterness only,
and I say to myself,
Just a little longer.

An owl peers down,
with a question in her eyes.
She doesn't have a hope,
in helping me,
as she doesn't see my pain,
spreads her wings,
passes me by,
and I say to myself,
Just a little longer.

The soft earth,
seems the only thing holding me up.
Even then I could slip,
and wondering takes me,
to why and how I got here,
without even knowing it.
Yet no one notices,
as they didn't see before,
so I say to myself,
Just a little longer.

Shimmering in the darkness,
I see two moons,
reflecting off a stream of thoughts,
ongoing forever more,
along a rocky road.
Slowly giving in to finding a way out,
I take the plunge under the river,
then the wind carries a whisper,
gently on a breeze,
'Just a little longer.'

In Heaven's Light

Graced amid an Angel's wing
to reach the stars and
catch the sky,
I place my prayers and greatest dreams
now blessed, in Heaven's Light.

Prayer

I pray for you and wish I could do more,
but more I cannot do from far away.
Like leaves before the wind we cannot stay,
Rippled dancing, dancing to the forest floor.
I wish I could your ailing health restore
and bring you to the strength of yesterday,
but all we mortal souls can do is pray
that God might alter what we have in store.
The beauty in our fragile life is love,
the only thing that makes the moment matter,
the golden thread that binds us all in light.
I wish, I wish I could your pain remove,
but like a wall the truth my will must shatter,
and so I send my prayers into the night.

May I Go?

May I go now?
Do you think the time is right?
May I say goodbye to pain filled days
and endless lonely nights?
I've lived my life and done my best,
an example tried to be.
So can I take that step beyond
and set my spirit free?
I didn't want to go at first,
I fought with all my might.
But something seems to draw me now
to a warm and living light.
I want to go,
I really do.
It's difficult to stay.
But I will try as best I can
to live just one more day.

To give you time to care for me
and share your love and fears.
I know you're sad and afraid,
because I see your tears.
I'll not be far,
I promise that, and hope you'll always know
that my spirit will be close to you
wherever you may go.
Thank you so for loving me,
you know I love you too.
That is why it's hard to say goodbye
to end this life with you.
So hold me now just one more time
and let me hear you say,
because you care so much for me,
will you let me go today?

Snap Shot

Pose for this picture,
I want to memorize your stare
because time passes by so fast
and it is becoming darker.

Write to me your words
running over and over again.
Etch your memory into my bedpost
with your fingernails.

Stain these vacant walls with your song,
hit them hard and leave your mark.
Throw your rainbow to the floor
let it soak and seep into the grains,
I will paint myself
into your portrait.
A twisted memory.

Maybe if I scream loud enough
I can keep the sun from setting.
Write my poems.
Add a few chapters to your dance.
For right now,
I wish to remember this,
as we pose for this picture.

LOSS

I look above and then below,
but there's no way that I can go.
I have no way to penetrate the endless and infinite sky,
to retrieve the remains of life.
In the world of torment they lie,
for my sword cannot slice the infinite sky.

Alone

Alone in the darkness,
step into the light.
The stars shine down
in the still of the night.
A seed in my mind
planted by love,
a white feather falls
from the wing of a dove.
The warmth of the stars
on a warm summer night,
the strength of the soul
in life's limelight.
Just a blur in my mind
like a stranger's dream,
my love will flow
at the burst of a seam.
Alone in my bed
now I know,
tonight is the night
I will let you go.

Eternity Between

A bleak gray stone stands upright on a naked patch of ground,
there is a couple dozen roses laying newly spread around.
A teardrop falls from where I stand
as I survey the memories
that lay beneath, hidden in the ground.

I look above and then below, but there's no way that I can go,
I have no way to penetrate the endless and infinite sky.
To retrieve the remains of life,
in the world of torment they lie,
for my sword can't slice the infinite sky.

I wish I had the power to throw a lifeline to the lifeless,
the spirit that screams in bloody cries of anguish.
But now it's too late, and my blind eyes see.
Six feet is so close to me,
but there's eternity in between.

Already Dead

Naked under a pale blue sky,
I watch the jets go by.
I wish I was up there,
going somewhere,
going nowhere,
going away.

Somewhere there is me,
here a life is torn.
If I could somehow
find all the pieces,
and sew them together,
maybe I'd be...

But I'm already dead,
and it's already lost,
and I already know
what I try to ignore.

The noose cannot be seen,
nor can it be felt,
but every day it grows tighter and tight,
with every though it steals my fight.

I used to think I was a kite,
that flew around the earth so high,
but pretty soon I realized,
what brings you up will let you die.

Then I have my wishes,
I have my dreams,
but from some forgotten space inside,
the laughter burns my heart.
I want to stay, to try again,
the seasons to defy,
but the fact burns brighter every day,
the minutes have no mercy.

Maybe if I had a gem,
a jewel I could never lose.
Maybe then the truth would change,
but I'm already dead,
and it's already lost,
and I already know
what I try to ignore.

It hurts too much to think,
too much to breathe,
too much to be,
to hang in a half-unconscious state.
It hurts to live in the barren cell,
it hurts to be invisible,
and maybe someday, somewhere, somehow?

But I already know,
that I am already dead,
everything is already lost
Far too much pain to ignore.

Darkness

I am swimming all alone in a pool of darkness,
I feel like darkness is slowly pulling me under.
I yell for help but no one is there to hear it.
I begin to see the water at eye level
and I kick and flail,
fighting to stay above the darkness,
but the darkness won't let go of its hold on me.
I slowly begin to give in
to the feeling that lies below the water line.
The waters starts to fill my lungs,
the lungs that once held so much life,
yet now they allow the murky water to replace that.
I know this path doesn't lead to happiness,
but why doesn't someone grab my hand
and pull me from darkness's grasp?
Because no one knows I stand at the boundary,
the boundary between light and dark,
so I give in to the thing that holds me.
All of the strength and all of the courage
that I once held in my heart
can't save me from the water.
So I slowly slip below the world of consciousness,
undetected by the occupants of that world.
I don't want to fight anymore,
I've given into darkness.

Knocking

Who is it knocking at my front door?
Is it the many lives that I have lived before?
Is it all my hopes, dreams, my prayers answered?
Or just the wind creating memories?
Must this become another dream?
Another sound that only I invented?
Have my tears sought so much beauty unanswered,
that the sound is only the tears dropping on the floor?

Is there a possibility that this sound
is a knocking at my door?
Is this the last sound I will hear before
my soul takes leave to return Home,
back from where I came?
Is this the sound of final judgment,
calling me home, where I can finally rest in peace?
Or is it you?

All that I have ever wanted,
searched for years.
Yet when I open the door when in my youth
the sound looked back and laughed at me.
Is it wrong to hope, to pray that it is you
that has come knocking?
I am so afraid that before I have a chance
to open the door the sound,
as you, will disappear.

If I Knew

If I knew it would be that last time
that I'd see you fall asleep,
I would tuck you in more tightly
and pray the Lord, your soul to keep.

If I knew it would be the last time
that I see you walk out the door,
I would give you hug and kiss
and call you back for one more.

If I knew it would be the last time
I'd hear your voice lifted up in praise,
I would video tape each action and word,
so I could play them back day after day.

For surely there's always tomorrow
to make up for an oversight,
and we always get a second chance
to make everything right.

There will always be another day
to say our "I love you's",
and certainly there's another chance
to say our "Anything I can do's."

But just in case I might be wrong,
and today is all I get,
I'd like to say how much I love you
and I hope we never forget,

Tomorrow is not promised to anyone,
young or old alike,
and today may be the last chance
you get to hold your loved one tight.

So if you're waiting for tomorrow,
why not do it today?
For if tomorrow never comes,
you'll surely regret the day,

That you didn't take the extra time
for a smile, a hug, or a kiss
and you were too busy to grant someone,
what turned out to be their one last wish.

So hold your loved ones close today,
and whisper in their ear,
that you love them very much and
you'll always hold then dear.

Take time to say "I'm sorry,"
"Please forgive me," "thank you," or "it's okay",
and if tomorrow never comes,
you'll have no regrets about today.

When sunlight spreads through forests
and picks up that still scent of trees,
then you come,
like a sailboat on the breeze.

When it floats down the cove
where boats lie tethered,
fog rises among them,
and you are on the path to the river.

When you come where violets bloom
at the edge of the meadow
and frogs sing their bass into
cricket sounds near the pond,
I'll be there,
wherever that is,
waiting for you.

She Weeps for Her Lover

A remembered song from
when love was strong,
reminds her that memories of love
have faded into love of memories.

Memories of love that slowly dissolve into
an unwanted and forgotten past.
An unwanted and forgotten
past that intrudes,
interrupts the present,
then invades the future.

The invaded future tries with its hope to nourish
and heal her broken heart.
A broken heart made tender by love and vulnerable
to severance and separation.

She seeks severance from the pain of a lost love,
and separation from the hurt of unfriendly eyes.
The tears and confusion conceal the strength of the
gentle spirit within, that will fill the heart once
again with love.

She weeps for her lover.

Night Cry

I cried to the Nightwind.
She did not know my name.
I called to the sky.
The stars would not shine.

I pleaded with the moon.
It passed unheeding.
I prayed to my gods.
Silence answered me.

I searched for you in all
the familiar places.
I looked in vain for your
face in all the crowds.

I watched you smile
in the corner of a memory.
I heard you laugh
in a remembered conversation.

I listened to your heart beat
through the muffled filter of time.
I danced with you in fantasy
of spontaneous choreography.

I waited for the dawn to evaporate
my anguish with the morning dew.
My heart almost burst with emotion but
my wait was in vain.

The sun rose, the dew taken,
and still, I stood in the morning sun,
waiting to grasp a hand
that was not there.

Loneliness

Slowly eating out my soul,
no one near, no hand to touch.
Will you help to make me whole?
My dear, I need you so much.

Heart poured out, accepted not,
wants and dreams I shared with you.
My desire is all I've got
for a man with the eyes of blue.

If this is too much to ask,
and hand and heart you cannot give,
then within your light I'll bask,
and with loneliness I'll live.

Possesses Me

My dreams wear thinner
as the years go by.

The strong face of fate is my own,
staring back in the mirror at her.

I stare back with a still face,
but not one of stone.

How hard the forgetting,
how easy the remembering.

How cruel is the process,
that possesses me.

Not For Burning

I come across your old letters,
the words still clinging to the page,
holding onto their places patiently,
with no intention of abandoning the white space.
They say that you will never leave me,
and reading them again I almost believe it,
but I suspect that they are heretics,
that later, in the fire, they will deny it all.

Then I remember something I once read,
as my memory is filled with voices of the dead
that it is a heretic which makes the fire,
and I am more guilty than your words.
Poor pilgrims who trusted the road your sent them down
and kept severely to the way. I forgive them;
I let them live to freely proclaim
what they thought would always be true.

Subconscious Whispers

My subconscious whispers in my dreams,
it calls your name in tortured screams.
Bewildered mind and vanquished heart,
I wish it would, this pain, depart.

But no, my mind won't let me be,
my heart, it just won't set me free.
I'm told to fight a battle lost,
a battle fought with utmost cost.

The light is gone, I've lost existence,
my soul is bound by absurd persistence.
I can't awake, the dream has control,
the phases of sleep: pain... then bitter cold.

It's almost as if I'm going to die,
the dream remains but the body still lies.
Again the cold has come and gone,
as I awake to yet another dawn.

I ask again as I've asked before,
Why, this pain, must I endure?

The Nest of Sleep

Sleep came and found me in pieces,
gathering me in it's nest.
Sweet smells in this eerie dream,
reality becomes soft.
I lie here shattered
for all of my waking lives.
Sleep and I will find sanctuary
in the holes we provide for each other.
As my Angel bones sprout wings,
claws of heightened consciousness
puncture this ethereal mating.
Begging to be left
in this slumbering oblivion.
Wakefulness outshines
the dark beauty of sleep,
bringing the sun
to the heat of my bed
and warm reality
to a temperature
I can
withstand.

Now I Can

I can have all the blankets
on this big bed now,
and keep books on the side
where you used to lie.

I can smoke cigarettes
if I want
and wear plaid
and turn the lights on bright
at 3 A.M. to write these words

But when the rain
comes pouring down
and a sparrow lights
close on the rail for refuge
and the petals of spring
fall softly to the ground

no eyes meet mine
in silent expectation,
sharing the moment
without saying a word.

When the Wind Blows

It tortures my insides.
Frustrated in my pain,
I am not sane.
I look in a mirror,
I watch myself die.

I laugh at a tear
as I watch as I cry.
Too many people are watching.
A dry wind is blowing,
cutting me like a knife.

I can feel the blood flowing
inside my veins.
I look in the sky
watching it cry
I dance in the rain.

All of my innocence
was taken away.
All of my fear
left inside to decay.
In this world I wonder
can I survive?

There is nothing left
to keep me alive.
Life is a choice,
I have chosen to live.
I have a voice that I choose to give.

All I can do now
is to stare at the wall.
I have nothing left
to do except to
Pray.

Last Kiss

You'll never know
when the last kiss will be,
when someone will fall
into their destiny.
Your lips faintly touched,
it may have been rushed,
but that's the last
that will ever be.

No Witness

If there is no sound
without a witness
to hear a tree fall
in the forest,
then how would you know
that I have cried,
when there are tears
falling from the heavens?

Sorrow

Sorrow is but a moment,
a tear that falls now and then,
a smile that is lost in the rainfall,
a pain that cries in your head.
Sorrow is but a moment,
a shadow that stands by your side,
a silence that speaks in anger,
a heart that only pities itself.
But it is only a moment;
breathe again and it will be gone,
for sorrow is only a moment
and a moment doesn't last very long.

Tim

I was cut off from you and could not piece
together bows that lay beyond your rain.
Weep, weep within me, darling. There's release
in knowing that your love, like magic fleece,
will warm me through the winters that remain.
You live inside of me, so rest in peace.
My love for you, my Tim, my Soul, will increase
as more and more of your will I will unchain.
Weep, weep within me, darling, there's release.
You live inside of me, so rest in peace.

MISSING YOU

As I whisper your name into the wind
and wait for my thoughts to bring you again,
I can only imagine you holding me tonight
and wait for the day that we reunite.

Anniversary

From the ruins of the night
I come home,
grateful that the sky has dressed
appropriately,
draping its mourning shawl over
the roof that was your faithful shelter.
I find courage to step inside.
I cannot turn on the light.
I cannot bear to see what I know is inside,
you're stuffed proud briefcase weighing
itself on the bathroom scale,
as if to remind me that it is more
tangible than you will ever be, again.

Instead I kick off my heels,
toss my coat to the bed,
lie down on the couch,
wishing I could sleep until it is night
once more or forever.

I refuse to let tears touch my cheeks tonight.
I am so afraid they will remind me of
your warm, soft mouth
and your soft blue eyes.

I will not try to think of yesterdays,
when you were alive.
I still lie, and think of the day ahead
when I will see you again.
I have always tried to be like you,
my love, and now,
I am trying harder than ever to
be as you are—
not seeing, not hearing, not smelling,
but most of all,
not feeling.

Capturing the Magic

I wonder silently
as I wander slowly
through this life
that was mine
and ours.

Now mine alone.

Our time was fleeting
within the whole picture
of life that is
behind me,
beside me,
ahead of me.

We tried hard
to capture the magic.
Not each and every time,
but more times than not
we succeeded.
Even in our failures
we realized
that
it was our trying
that mattered the most.

Just a Little Note

To say that I love you.
To say that I miss your soft hair.
To say that these days I spend apart from you
are the hardest days of my life.

Just a little note

To let you know I think of you.
To let you see how much I care about you.
To let my heart speak what little comfort
to you I can offer.

Just a little note

That speaks of my joy.
That carries you my dreams.
That tells you that no matter how far away
you are, I will never be more then a thought away.

Just a little note

To say I love you.

One or Two?

Feeling as though our new love is abating,
dying to embers before it can flame.
Shattering memories we were creating,
still my heart aches at the sound of your name.

Wanting and cherishing changes you're bringing,
trying to understand all of your needs.
Love songs to you I had just begun singing,
tossed from the pathways of Love, my heart bleeds.

Tell me I'm wrong, that these thoughts have no meaning,
wipe away tears beginning to fall.
Silence the sad dirge of death my heart's keening,
know love can't run 'til it learns to crawl.

Keep me beside you, inside you in your heart,
strengthen those feelings that I thought lay dead.
Balm of my soul, give me time to do my part.
Hold me in your arms and vanquish my dread.

Tonight

I can only imagine you holding me tonight,
as you take my fear and seal my fright.
I can only dream of the look in your eyes,
as I forget it's not real and deny its lies.
I can only hope someday it will be true,
and I will feel the strength that is you.

As I whisper your name into the wind
and wait for my thoughts to bring you again,
then I remember I can only imagine you holding me tonight
and wait for the day you keep me tight.
I can only remember the look in your eyes,
because the rest is a blur my soul unties.

My dreams, wishes, and memories,
I sustain them until your arms are around me again.
I can cope with the pain.
Forever in my heart you will be holding me tight,
even if I have to only imagine you holding me tonight.

Trapped

Bottled up inside,
are the words I never said,
the feelings that I hide,
the lines you never read.
You can see it in my eyes,
read it in my face,
trapped inside are lies,
of the past I can't replace.
Memories that hold to my heart
won't seem to go away.
Why can't I make a new start?
Today's a brand new day.

Yesterdays are over,
even thought the hurting is not.
Nothing lasts forever.
Don't take my love for granted,
for soon it will all be gone.
All I ever wanted
was the love you thought you'd won.
The hurt I'm feeling now,
will not disappear overnight.

No more wishing for the past.
It wasn't meant to be,
It didn't seem to last,
so I have to set it free.

With One Heart

It was night.
The eyes of heaven stared down
to the two of us on the ground.
Serenity.
I was wet with dew
as I sat with you.
Vivacious.
My thoughts skipped round in the clouds,
where we danced around.
Beautiful.
You were beautiful when we danced,
were beautiful as we danced,
be beautiful again.
Wonderful.
You were wonderful when with me,
be wonderful again.

If it had not come, if you had not died,
would you have stayed with me, with one heart?
Stayed by my side, kept me alive,
given yourself to only one heart?

Wishing Back to a Time

Until the sunlight has stopped her weeping,
through shattered green and cracks of grey,
and teary drops on morning rising, that seem once cold,
to fall unaided from Aurora's sleeping face,
I'll dance again in silent dreaming,
wrapped in darkened embers,
until the sun touches the sleeping bay,
a morning that time remembers.
Slipping silently on a starlit dream,
seeing things that only Time can see.
Waiting in the darkness patiently
for a voice,
tone unchanged by ears first hearing,
and words unguarded by spotlights shining.

From the Distance of Our Separation

From the distance of our separation
I see the whole of which I was a part;
I see the way my temper tore your heart,
then the love beneath the laceration.
I see the landscape shaping our relation:
Your fear that I might choose with little art,
my anger at the dreams you would impart,
the ancient paths that lead to confrontation.
But knowledge needn't linger in regret,
nor wait upon some wind to clear its sky.
We are none the worse for what is gone.
The moments that I never will forget
are those whose careless grace must make me cry,
safe within a heart forever won.

Void

Void, canceled, simply annulled.
Endlessly aching, unconsoled.
Life without you, cause without reason.
Touch without sense, time without season.
Life faced now like a cancerous sore,
a sordid parasite that eats at my core.
All that makes me whole, all I hold deep within,
leaving me lifeless, or at least not 'living'.

A shallow face anguished and marred.
An empty space scaled and scarred.
Sweetly abiding to a cynical charade.
Secretly hiding 'hind a fictitious facade.
Still, lost within this heart of glass,
this fragile and yet unfeeling mass
lies the remains of a love that glowed,
the gift to you I once bestowed.

But honor and pride now bereaved
by your love for me so misconceived.
Ripped from my inner depths, impeding,
mind, body and spirit, bleeding,
now's crushed to sand from thy ruthless hand,
a cold stare I just can't understand.
I feel that somehow, somehow I'm dying,
at least my soul and all that's underlying.

A simple void, is that what I've become?
The hollowed sphere on a pendulum.
Swinging back and forth, emotion to emotion,
never once stopping, nor slowing the motion.
No reason, no answer, no justification.
the creation of a sterile imagination.
Just passing through time as time passes me.
Merely a nothing, nothing, merely left to be.

Sightless and soundless, unseen and unheard.
Mindless and boundless, obscure and absurd.
All empathy lying unlaced, unemployed,
I live my life dying, unembraced, in a void.

MEMORIES

Deep in niches of our hearts,
safe from the erosion
of time and circumstance,
in the precious marble of memory,
we sculpted our first embrace.

Forever Searching

I search for you through it all,
through the endless storms of tears and skies of darkness.
I only search for you, forever and always you,
you are everything and nothing.
You are invisible to my shielded eyes and endless dreams,
you are a puddle in the desert which I cannot find,
you are an arm stretching out which I cannot reach.
You're the air I breathe.
The unforgettable memories are of you,
always and only you,
for you are the love in my broken heart,
the strength in my condemned soul.
You are my everything, the nothing,
you are the face I can't forget.
I've searched so very far and I've searched wide,
I searched everywhere
for a reminiscent part of you,
and found none.
I feel your presence in it all,
in the wind, the sun
in warmth, and in bitter cold.
You're always there by my side
and in my heart,
places you've yet to disappear
and hopefully never will.

Audience of One

When your heart is singing
a song only one person can hear,
it is beautiful when you listen,
even for a moment.

For in that one moment of listening
the notes of the song then
become a melody and
the melody creates a memory.

Your Name

I will put my red lips together,
pursing them around the folds of your name,
gently caressing your memory.
In tears and in pain
I will put my red lips together,
bring my hand to them
to cover the emotion,
I cannot restrain.
The emotion of love and distain.

My Love

I will hum my love a melody
with no words, for words cannot convey.
The love I feel in notes will come,
where words would get in the way.

I will paint my love a work of art,
no brush or paint would do.
I will use a rainbow from the sky,
to make the love shine through.

I will write my love a sonnet,
with neither pen or lines.
The cadence is my heartbeat,
the feeling needs no rhyme.

I will give my love a memory,
for memories are true.
They need no words, brush or pen,
but are always with you.

Rome

As I walk these streets
of Rome in the springtime,
accompanied by the ghosts
of Augustine and Keats
we watch the children and the pigeons
dancing in the plaza,
accompanied by the street players
on flutes and mandolins.

The facades and the fountains
and marble-muscled statues
watch with us
in silent contemplation
the rousing and spinning,
the roaring and the dinning
of the flower-spangled plaster-peeling
glory that is Rome.

The Angels

The angels are crying for they feel my broken heart.
They flutter around my soul trying to protect it from you.
You fooled the angels for they never thought us to be apart.
The angels are angered by your insensitive attitude.
The angels are sighing when they watch my tears fall at night.
They talk among themselves but can't fix what you've done.
The angels have no mercy and want you out of sight.
They don't want to listen to you and find you quite tiresome.
The angels shield me from the uncertain future ahead.
They promise me that with time I will begin to heal.
The angels are warning you to watch where you tread.
The angels form a circle and protect me from your will.

Thoughts of Love

The simple thoughts of one you love
like raindrops on a fertile ground
can bring to you a fresh breeze
and rainbows too, spread all around.

It is within your heart you find
a world of peacefulness and song.
Yes! In your heart and in your soul
the thoughts of loving cannot be wrong.

His Blue Eyes

I miss his blue eyes,
the way they shone and glistened.
The way every time he whispered,
angels stopped to listen.

I miss his blue eyes singing,
always out of tune,
the hills and all our talking,
fumbling under the moon.

I miss his blue eyes laughing
at jokes that weren't that funny.
The way he'd wear his shirt,
how he wasted all of his money.

I miss his blue eyes dancing,
his two left feet on fire,
how he'd light the room,
how he would never tire.

I miss his blue eyes stories,
how he read my poems line by line.
Crossed his heart, said he would not die,
though he did in time.

I miss his blue eyes soaring,
through my body late at night.
I miss the way we broke the morning,
the way we stole the night.

I miss his blue eyes smiling,
how the future seemed to shine.
I miss his blue eyes kissing
me with every move.

I miss him all the time.

Marble Marble

Deep in niches of our hearts,
safe from the erosion
of time and circumstance,
in the precious marble of memory
we sculpted our first embrace.

LOVE FROM ABOVE

In the heart of God your life still exists
but it's you, my love, that I can't resist.
As the heavens part I see you so clear,
from the warmth in my heart I feel you so near.

Love From Above

Send me to Heaven
I pray,
when I no longer use my body rightfully,
when my limbs can't bear my weight
and dignity is stripped by fate.
Look into my eyes, you will find a tired soul,
I will let you know, it's time.
You must help me from this edge.
Now it's time, I make this pledge.
I leave you for Heaven today.
Anew, I run, I laugh, I am whole!
We shared a life of grandness.
To your heart my leaving brings,
the pain of loss, I feel that too,
but know, this I must do.
I must leave first, to make the way
for you to follow me someday.

Beyond the sunset, where all pain ends,
we will meet again, I will wait for you.
Just as I snuggled in your heart,
you are in mine too, we are never apart.
I now watch you from afar and pray.
It will take time to heal,
yet you will heal some each day.
Please dry those tears and smile for me,
know at last that I am free.
There is no pain or suffering here.
The sun shines brightly everywhere.
There isn't even one cross look,
it's not allowed here in His book.
No clouds of gray will gather here,
no storms will ever threaten.
We are at peace here,
and bring you complete love from above.

Angel Wings

Wrap around Her your Angel Wings,
And keep Her safe tonight.
While she walks, all by herself,
please be a shining light.

Keep Her warm when the cold winds blow,
and lift Her gentle brown hair.
Keep Her comforted, Angel Wings,
for tonight I can't be there.

Give Her peace, please, Angel Wings,
tonight, when she gets home.
Let Her feel your gentle weight,
tonight while I am gone.

Rest Her head on your angel feathers,
when tonight, she falls asleep.
Hear my prayers and take them in,
for I pray Her soul you keep.

Angel Wings, when she wakes up,
and starts another day,
keep Her company in every moment,
as long as I'm away.

And let Her know, that in my life,
she is everything that I live for.
If you, Angel Wings, can grant me this,
what else could I ask for?

Let Her smile Her Angels smile,
as She lives day by day.
Let Her see the endless love from me
that will never go away.

And, Angel Wings, will you let Her hear,
those words that hurt Her heart:
A simple "I Love You", or another "I'm sorry",
for being so far apart.

Wrap around Her your Angel Wings,
and keep Her safe for life.
She is more than priceless to me,
so be Her constant right.

Keep Her warm when the cold winds blow,
and let Her know how I care.
Keep Her in total comfort, Angel Wings,
in Her life when I can't be there.

December Night

On a crystal clear December night,
towards the heavens appeared a light,
casting colors of red, blue and green,
the most beautiful sight I had ever seen.
Feelings suddenly came over me,
of happiness, love and serenity.
As I stood there watching from afar,
the light changed into a beautiful star.
Shining so brightly down on me,
I suddenly realized what this could be.
For you see, last year on this very day
My loving Tim had passed away.

As I Sit

As I sit by my window
watching the stars,
I feel you beside me, touching me.
We've been separated by so many
miles, for such a long time.
And yet, I can feel one warm
ray in the infinite sky,
as we both reach for the same star,
and touch.

Night Dreams

As night descends upon the land,
you come to me in my dreams,
offering your hand.
In turn I offer you my heart.
All I ever want from you
is for us to never part.
But once again, as I turn to you,
you start to fade away.
Then I open my eyes and see,
it's the light of day.
All day long I'll wait
for night to come upon the land,
so that once again as I sleep,
you can offer me your hand.

A Bridge Called Love

It takes us back to brighter years, to happier sunlit days,
to precious moments that will be with us always.
These fond recollections are treasured in the heart,
to bring us always close to those, from whom we had to part.
There is a bridge of memories from earth to Heaven above,
it keeps our dear ones near to us.
It is the bridge that we call "love".

The Dream

In the whisper of a heart beat
he was here.
So real, his memory deep within my soul.
I won't ask why he had come.
He looked so real, his face so fine.
Heaven has been good to him.
His eyes holding back the tears,
his arms reach for me.

Don't take away this moment!
Dear God, you have given him to me.
Oh dance with me once again.
Dance the dance of echo's past,
God, don't break the spell,
please leave me be!

Then I awakened,
he was gone,
I was alone.

Fly Away

Fly away on golden wings,
far from all these mortal things.

Fly to where the Angels live,
see the beauty Heaven gives.

Fly away from darkness, night,
fly away and find the light.

Fly away your life is done,
your endless journey has begun.

But hold your memories bittersweet,
until once again we meet.

Fly away on golden wings,
your heart is pure, your soul will sing.

Fly on the other shore,
where there is peace forevermore.

The White Feather

This pain that I feel, it's so deep in my heart.
It hurts me so much when we're so far apart.
The pain from your love, I feel it's so strong.
I ask you, my Lord, what have I done wrong?

In the heart of God your life still exists,
but it's you, my love, that I can't resist.
As the heavens part, I see you so clear
and your warmth in my heart, I feel you so near.

The whispers of angels that play in the dark
are like children that play at a nearby park.
They laugh and they sing and float in the skies
as I search for you with tears in my eyes.

Why, my dear Lord, have you taken him home
when you gave us this planet and freedom to roam?
What is this message that you want me to see?
For why shall I live without him to be?

Our lives are so short without all this pain,
as short as the whisper from an angel in vain,
like waves on the seashore that fold on the sand,
and the sound of your thunder that bolts from your hand.

I've sat all alone in the dark with my fears.
My eyes, they still heave without all the tears.
I've looked to the heavens to understand thee.
If not for him, Lord, why not then take me?

I look in the mirror and I see a trace
of the one that I miss and his beautiful face.
My days are my nights and my nights are my days,
your stars shine like sunshine with powerful rays.

Your gift of your giving has a price we all pay,
his memory will last forever, forever and a day.
I know that he is safe in your giving heart,
it is I who must find a brand new start.

The angels I see who come out to play,
they play in the darkness in my sunshiny day.
They hold him so close and love his so sweet,
it warms up my soul and my heart skips a beat.

I still look for him every now and then.
You've changed all our lives, we no longer pretend.
I see him at times as he is heaven-bound,
as a white feather gently falls to the ground.

With You In My Dreams

I thought that you were still in love with me
last night while I slept.
As we walked through meadows golden and free,
pleasant thoughts through my head crept.
Sweet with sleep, inside my head
you were alight with heaven's beams,
and though I was asleep in bed,
I was with you in my dreams.
When I need to, want to, have to see you
and am ripping apart at the seams,
closing my eyes is all I must do
to visit you in my dreams.
I fear sleep may escape me tonight,
after all my excitement and schemes,
but with you as my calm, I will never know fright
when I see you this night in my dreams.
As long as the earth meets the sea
and comets have tails of gossamer streams,
I will remember you, and we
will be together in my dreams.

The North Star

Viewing the North Star,
I close my eyes and I feel the moon rise.
The night enfolds me, I welcome
the darkness with its mystical ways,
drifting on lustrous streams, wrapped
in a perfume of splendor.
I feel your presence,
I weave your name into my dreams.
I tie the golden threads,
once more compelled to surrender.
Morning returns to me soon,
yet dim with another day's tears.
Outside my window the
roses cry with the morning dew.
They cry to live. I cry for you.

You Came to Me in My Sleep

You told me in a dream you always loved me.
I wept with joy at what you said.
My sadness was not there. It was so lovely.
I was with you was my darling, although you are dead.
The sky was with an early sunrise burning,
yet still with ample darkness for the moon,
which held the secret of its youthful yearning,
although it knew that it would vanish soon.
How wonderful, I thought, at last to hear you
say what I had known, but never heard!
Abandoned, I have longed to be near you
and find my long-lost refuge in a word.
I saw the truth of it within your eyes,
and blessed the dream that ends, but never dies.

A Simple Thank You, My Angel

Into the dim lit, bare walls of my world,
you entered, bringing light and life to me.
The vivid colors, painted with a swirl
of wit and charm, of personality.
With tender care, you added comfort, warmth,
and images that line the now bright walls.
I look upon them fondly, bringing forth
a thankfulness that you walk in these halls
with me; our friendship has become a part
of my world now; it has its special place.
Within my being, my life, and in my heart,
your name hangs right beside your smiling face.
Remembering just how drab these walls had been,
I have to thank you for the light, my friend.

Wedding Blessing

When the sun rises
in the mornings of our life together,
remember the birth of your love.
When the sun sets
in the evenings of your journey,
remember the compassion of your heart.

Just as the heavens announce
the birth of a star,
celebrate your love,
created from a long lineage of love.
When one flame is joined with another,
a third flame is created
that is more intense,
and brighter, than either of the separate flames.

May each of you tend the flame,
for your union symbolizes
the ongoing process of spiritual creation.
May your bodies be comforted
from the warmth,
and may your spirits be renewed by the light of this flame.

May the light from this sacred love
illuminate the shadows
in the darkest chambers of your hearts.
When your spirit is wounded,
may the nurturing stillness of your love
guide you to your inner strength,
to heal your Spirit and mend your heart.

May the fire of your love
refine you and not consume you.
When you behold your beloved,
treasure the bond you have
as the most sacred gift of your days.